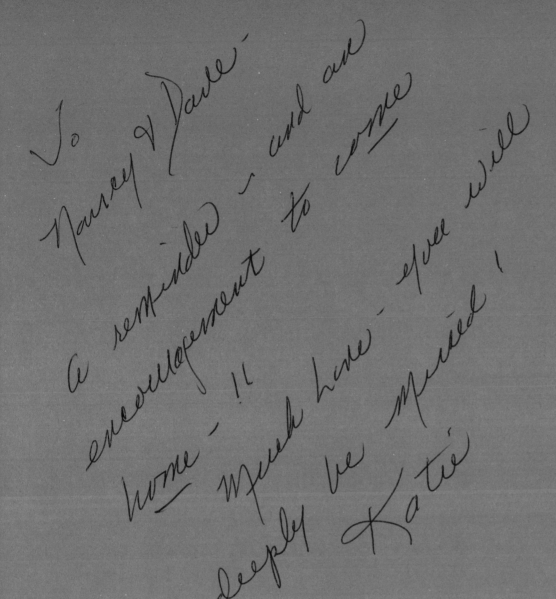

To
Nancy & Dave -
a reminder - and an
encouragement to come
home - !! - you will
- Much love - you will
deeply be Missed !
Katie

ORANGE COUNTY
portrait of a place

ANITA L. MAYA

Captions by RACHEL MAYA

GRAPHIC ARTS BOOKS

Library of Congress Control Number: 2006939027
International Standard Book Number: 978-0-88240-663-3

Book compilation © 2007 by
Graphic Arts Books, an imprint of
Graphic Arts Center Publishing Company
P.O. Box 10306, Portland, Oregon 97296-0306
503/226-2402; www.gacpc.com

The five-dot logo is a registered trademark of
Graphic Arts Center Publishing Company.

President: Charles M. Hopkins
Associate Publisher: Douglas A. Pfeiffer
Editorial Staff: Timothy W. Frew, Kathy Howard, Jean Bond-Slaughter
Production Coordinator: Heather Doornink
Cover Design: Elizabeth Watson
Interior Design: Jean Andrews

Printed in the United States of America

FRONT COVER: ◖ Long considered the jewel of Orange County's
coastal communities, Laguna Beach sweeps down from its populated hills to
artsy Laguna Village, where galleries stand just a volleyball toss from the sea.
BACK COVER: ◖ Turn-of-the-century bank and commerce buildings flank the center-
piece of Old Towne Orange, a traffic circle complete with fruit-laden orange trees.
◄◄ One of the most significant wetlands in California, the three-hundred-
acre Bolsa Chica Ecological Reserve glistens on a moonlit night.
◄ This section of Huntington Beach welcomes man's best friend.
► Once a rich hunting ground for Native Americans, Bolsa
Chica attracts migrating flocks from the Pacific Flyway.

◄ Thoughtfully developed, the city of Newport Beach
includes seven picturesque residential islands with one-of-a-kind
designer homes and more than nine thousand yachts and pleasure boats.
▲ Placed on the National Register of Historic Places in 1979, Crystal Cove
Historic District is a seaside enclave of early twentieth-century beach cottages.
►► In the westernmost corner of Orange County, the gateway city of Seal Beach
retains its charming small-town atmosphere on tree-lined Main Street.

◄ Basins of stone are sculpted smooth by time and tide at
Big Corona State Beach. Abundant tide pools are favorites for school
outings, nature enthusiasts, and families exploring marine life at the shore.

▲ CLOCKWISE FROM TOP LEFT: ● Thousands of weekend revelers attend the
Sand Castle Competition held every September on Big Corona State Beach.
● Whimsical and elaborate creations are fashioned from sand, shell, and water.
● The sometimes humorous creations remain until high tide washes them away.

▲ Narrower than most Orange County beaches,
Capistrano Beach offers biking, surfing, and fishing
along with a friendly small-town atmosphere.

▲ A landmark since 1928, the
San Clemente Pier is world renowned for
surf fishing, breathtaking views, and the ever-present
backdrop of the tiled-roof town of San Clemente.

▲ Two hundred stores, forty restaurants, two food courts, and year-round entertainment draw discriminating shoppers to Newport's Fashion Island.
▶ No trip to Balboa is complete without a visit to Dad's Original Ice Cream Stand, home of the delectable Balboa Bar and the world-famous chocolate-dipped Frozen Banana.

SINCE 1945

the Original Frozen Banana

ICE CRE
BALBOA

◄ Stocked with fish and perfect for swimming,
the man-made Lake Mission Viejo is the members-only
playground of an exclusive community of multimillion-dollar homes.
▲ The seaside community of Seal Beach is a popular surfing destination.
At 1,865 feet, its wooden pier is the second longest in California.

▲ Once nothing more than a sleepy community
known for its sun-bleached surfers and ramshackle surf
shops, Huntington Beach is en route to becoming a resort destination.
▶ Officially known as Dog Beach, this mile-long stretch of sand is one of
the few beachside havens permitting canines and their
owners to frolic in the sun and surf.

◀ Seal Beach's extra-deep stretch of
sand has room enough for sun worshippers, joggers,
kite flyers, boogie boarders, surfers, and even an occasional seagull.
▲ ALL IMAGES: ◗ Local artists create ornaments and knickknacks using
starfish and other sea creatures. Beginning at the pier, shoppers, tourists,
and souvenir hunters can stroll along Seal Beach's colorful Main
Street and find restaurants, gift shops, and even a tearoom.

21

▲ Shops full of surf-themed trinkets offer some-
thing for everyone on Seal Beach's tree-lined Main Street.
▶ Its southwest-facing beaches and nationwide reputation
as an excellent place to surf make Huntington Beach
the thriving hub of California's surfing industry.

◄ Considered one of Orange County's safest cities, the quality of life in
Huntington Beach is also enhanced by its health-conscious, outdoor lifestyle.
▲ With more than eight miles of pristine coastline, Huntington Beach
has hosted surf competitions for more than seventy years,
earning it the nickname of "Surf City U.S.A."

▲ Colorful paddles decorate beachside kiosks from Sunset Beach to Newport.
▶ On any given day in every kind of weather, kayakers,
surfers, boogie boarders, windsurfers, and pleasure
boaters take to the blue waters of the Pacific.

◄ Bolsa Chica State Ecological Reserve features
a 1.5-mile-long trail loop around a placid water inlet.
Perfect for studying local and migrating birds, the reserve is a
favorite spot for schoolchildren and nature conservationists.
▲ Nearly two hundred bird species are documented
in Bolsa Chica each year, including many
rare and endangered species.

◄ The footbridge and the trail off Pacific Coast Highway are
the best places to observe Bolsa Chica wildlife. Great blue herons,
snowy egrets, and brown pelicans are increasingly a common sight.
▲ Spotted almost exclusively alone in the past, the California
brown pelican now comes to the Bolsa Chica
wetlands in groups of three and four.

▲ Popular with railroad enthusiasts, the
Fullerton Station has two historic depots on site,
both on the National Register of Historic Places.

▲ Historically a center of agriculture, Fullerton was founded
in 1887 and named for the man who secured the local land rights
on behalf of the Atchison, Topeka and Santa Fe Railroad.

▲ Opened in Yorba Linda in 1990, the Nixon Library and Birthplace is dedicated to educating the public about the life and times of the nation's thirty-seventh president, and encouraging interest in history, government, and civic affairs.
▶ The nine-acre institution is a walk-through memoir featuring a museum, galleries, the First Lady's Garden, and the president's faithfully restored 1910 birthplace.
▶▶ Westminster's Little Saigon is a center of the county's Vietnamese community.

◀ Signs highlight the offerings at the Asian Garden Mall,
touted as the mall that never closes, even on traditional holidays.
▲ CLOCKWISE FROM TOP LEFT: ● Three giant marble deities watch over the mall's
main entrance. Gods of Happiness, Longevity, and Prosperity bless all who enter here.
● More than four hundred shops sell everything from toys to baked goods to antiques.
● The mall's upper level is the perfect place to find baubles of gold, jade, and precious stones.
● A reclining Buddha welcomes customers at one of the many shops in the mall.

39

▲ Founded in 1955 by Robert Schuler, the
Crystal Cathedral was designed by Philip Johnson. Ten
thousand rectangular panes of glass are incorporated in the design.
▶ The Crystal Cathedral is Garden Grove's majestic centerpiece. Home to the
world-renowned "Glory of Christmas" holiday pageant, the church is
also known for its 280 rank, five-manual (keyboard) pipe organ.

◄ The fountain and courtyard of the Bowers
Museum reflect California Mission architectural style.
▲ Internationally celebrated, the Bowers Museum is Orange County's
largest art museum. Featuring many world-class exhibitions, the Bowers is the
first museum outside of England to showcase collections from London's British Museum.
►► Wave action all along the coast provides perpetual entertainment.

43

▲ Santa Ana's Discovery Science Center is guarded by a
huge dinosaur skeleton that stretches halfway around the building.
► With more than one hundred hands-on exhibits, the Discovery Science
Center is partially housed in a ten-story solar cube, which
provides a percentage of the Center's energy needs.

◄ Santa Ana, Orange County's
government seat still retains its Spanish
and Mexican flavor, clearly evident in the city's place-
names like Plaza Fiesta, a favorite downtown gathering spot.
▲ One of America's foremost producers of new plays, Costa
Mesa's South Coast Repertory Theater is a focal point of
Orange County's cultural and entertainment life.

▲ Discriminating shoppers find the
perfect mix of retail, dining, and entertainment
at Fashion Island, Newport Beach.

▲ Fashion Islands' Mediterranean-themed carousel
features scenes of Venice on its rounding board above, and
whimsical animals styled from antique figures below.

▲ The Balboa Peninsula has been home to the famous
Balboa Pavilion since 1906, as well as the Balboa Fun Zone, a local
institution since 1936. The family-run Balboa Island Ferry has shuttled
both cars and people between Balboa Peninsula and Balboa Island since 1919.

▶ One of the largest small-boat harbors in the United States, Newport
Beach unfolds along six scenic miles of Orange County coastline.

◄ Multimillion-dollar mansions top the
chaparral-covered bluffs above Newport Beach.
▲ LEFT TO RIGHT: ◖ A refuge of rural charm, the Orange County
equestrian community is sandwiched beween Newport Beach and Costa Mesa.
◖ Hundreds of miles of bike routes and a favorable climate make the county ideal for cycling.
►► Once sold as swampland at a dollar an acre, Harbor, Balboa, and Lido islands are
now considered among the most desirable real estate in Southern California.

◄ Upper Newport Bay provides six diverse habitats
for more than two hundred bird species. One of the few
remaining wetlands in Southern California, the bay's 892 acres
include not only wetlands but also surrounding upland habitats.
▲ Known as one of the premier birding sites in North America,
these protected coastal wetlands are reminiscent of
long-ago Southern California landscapes.

▲ Crystal Cove Historic District features
forty-six vintage cottages on 12.3 acres of coastal land
within the almost three-thousand-acre Crystal Cove State Park.
▶ Undeveloped woodlands, a designated underwater park, tide pools, sandy
coves, and 3.5 miles of beach make Crystal Cove a unique
place to explore reefs, ridges, and canyons.

◄ Originally built to give residents easy access to
the beach, the Goldenrod Footbridge was erected in 1928,
stretching 243 feet over what was then known as Pacific Gulch.
▲ Framed by cliffs and a rock jetty that forms the east entrance to
Newport Harbor, Corona Del Mar State Beach is popular
with surfers, swimmers, and sunbathers.

▲ Little Corona Marine Life Refuge
is a protected area created to preserve the
animals and plants that make the tide pools their home.
▶ One of the last remaining examples of Southern California coastal
development, the conservancy of Crystal Cove has restored
numerous cottages back to their original 1920s charm.

◄ Just off Pacific Coast Highway, a steep stairway
follows the bluffs down to a footbridge at Los Trancos
Creek, where all roads lead to Crystal Cove's Historic District.
▲ A museum of living plants displayed in an intimate garden, the Sherman
Library and Gardens is Corona Del Mar's prized horticultural retreat.

▲ LEFT TO RIGHT: ◗ The cool atmosphere of the fern
grotto, one of several botanical collections within Sherman
Library and Gardens, provides a perfect respite in summer months.
◗ A lush greenhouse behind the walls of Corona Del Mar's Sherman Library
and Gardens makes a sultry home for a pond of golden and spotted koi.
▶ Wide brick walkways link areas of the garden while a patriotic
otter keeps water flowing in one of the courtyard fountains.

◄ The Mediterranean enclave of Corona Del Mar exudes small-town appeal
and offers views of nearby Newport Harbor, Balboa Peninsula, and Catalina Island.
▲ Designated as an underwater park featuring forests of kelp and unusual marine
life, Crystal Cove is actually seven separate coves along 3.5 miles of beach.
►► Researchers come to the Sherman Library where materials about
the history of the Pacific Southwest have been preserved since 1955.

▲ Old Towne Orange attracts architecture aficionados, antique collectors, and weekend browsers.
► CLOCKWISE FROM TOP LEFT: ◖ A favorite Hollywood stand-in for small-town America, the City
of Orange retains its charm on the busy sidewalks of its business district and residential streets.
◖ Hot shaving cream and straight razors are still the norm at old-fashioned Ray's Barber Shop.
◖ Antique shops and indoor flea markets piled with merchandise sit side by side with ethnic
restaurants, microbreweries, and English tearooms in historic Old Towne Orange.

◄ More than twenty-five thousand students
call UC Irvine home, making this Orange County
campus among the fastest-growing schools in the UC system.
▲ With an annual economic impact of nearly four billion dollars, UC
Irvine is Orange County's second-largest employer.

▲ With Laguna Beach's gorgeous hills and
long ribbon of open beach, this resort town and
artist colony with a pedestrian-friendly environment
draws millions of visitors throughout the year.

▲ Perfect year-round climate, unspoiled waters, and
a casual ambience are just a few of the charms that make
Laguna Beach a magnet for tourists and locals alike.

79

▲ Surfers, boogie boarders, and swimmers
share seven miles of Laguna's pristine coastline with
dolphins, pelicans, and the occasional California sea lion.
▶ Nestled between the sea and a gentle range of coastal hills, the
colorful beach colony of Laguna was put on the map in
1932 by its world-famous Pageant of the Masters.

◄ Swimming, surfing, skin diving, and fishing are popular pastimes
where Aliso Creek winds down from the Laguna foothills and empties into the sea.
▲ From 1900 to the late 1940s, Aliso Beach was a privately owned campground. In the 1960s,
the County of Orange acquired the beachfront and inland property up to Aliso Creek.
►► More than fifty galleries, numerous restaurants, and dozens of high-end
boutiques serve the local and tourist trade in downtown Laguna Village.

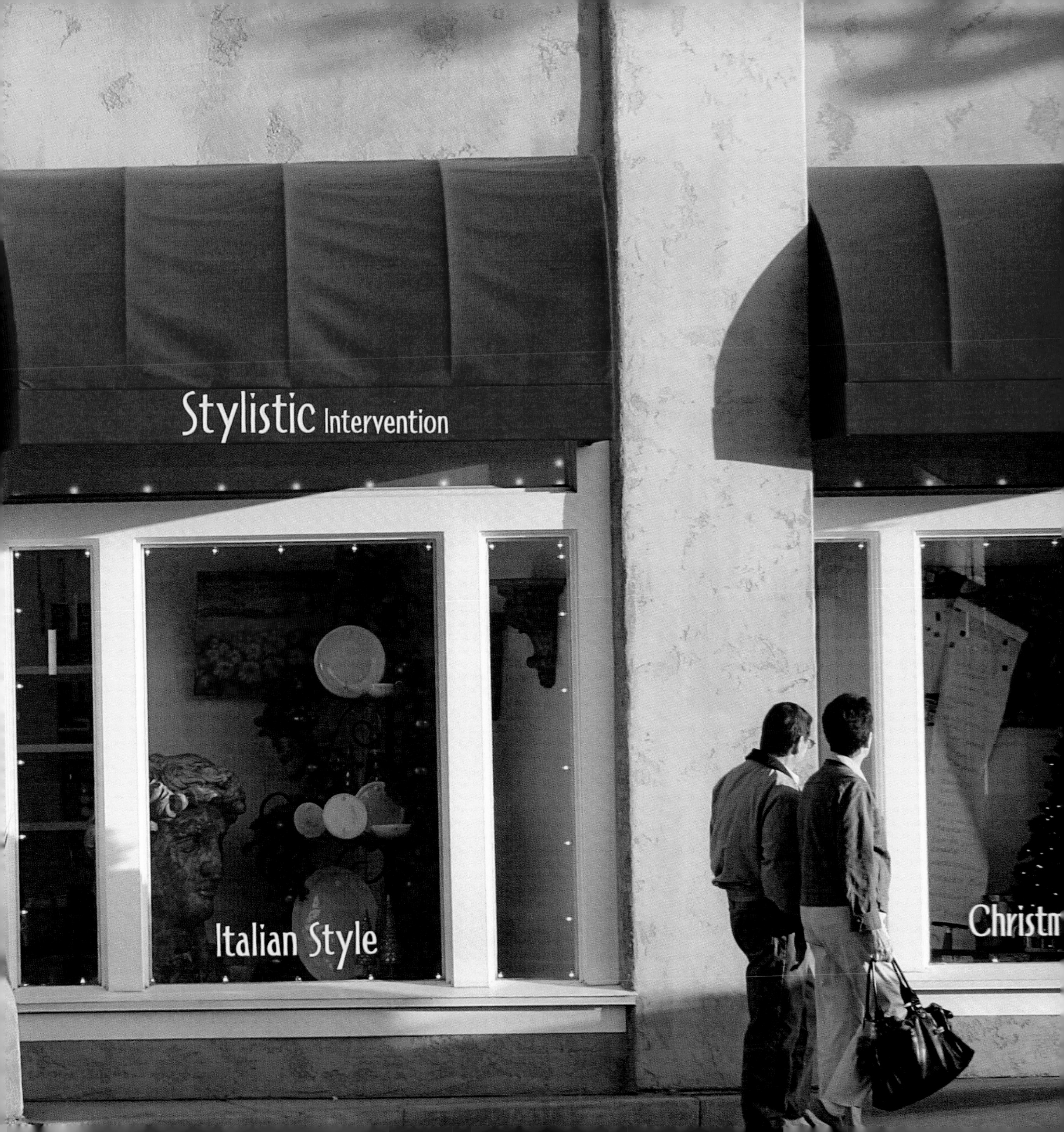
Stylistic Intervention
Italian Style

▲ Long a haven for writers, artists, and Hollywood stars,
Laguna Beach is home to all things artistic, beautiful, and decorative.
► Not far from Laguna Beach's business district, manicured bluffs and residential
hills provide a rich backdrop to the exquisite blue crescent of coast.

◄ Built in 1928, the San Clemente Pier was heavily
damaged during the storms of 1983. Rebuilt and improved,
the 1,296-foot-long pier is a popular Orange County fishing spot.

▲ LEFT TO RIGHT: ◗ Once a boundary between the Juaneno and Gabrieleno tribes,
Aliso Creek and its salt marshes played an important role in Orange County's early history.

◗ Keeping this man-made body of water safe for swimming is a daily accomplishment.
Water quality is regularly checked at each of Lake Mission Viejo's private beaches.

▲ One of the most picturesque communities in
Southern California, Laguna Beach is a colorful blend
of the spiritual, artistic, dramatic, and sporting lifestyles.

▶ Like a picture postcard from another era, the panoramic vistas of
Capistrano Beach evoke unforgettable memories of Orange County's past.

▶▶ Another gem along California's sun-kissed Riviera, Capistrano Beach is a
sixty-two-acre paradise of clean ocean, outdoor sports, and relaxation.

90

◀ Named after Richard Henry Dana Jr.,
author of *Two Years Before the Mast*, Dana Point's
narrow beach is home to a replica of Dana's brig, *Pilgrim*.
▲ During the nineteenth century this rugged cove,
then called Bahia Capistrano, served as the major
port between San Diego and Santa Barbara.

95

The sign on the monument reads:

DANA POINT

NAMED FOR RICHARD HENRY DANA, AUTHOR OF "TWO YEARS BEFORE THE MAST," WHO WAS HERE IN 1835. EL EMBARCADERO, THE COVE BELOW, WAS USED BY HIDE VESSELS TRADING WITH MISSION SAN JUAN CAPISTRANO. THIS TRADE REACHED ITS PEAK IN 1830 - 1840. HERE IN 1818 HIPOLITO BOUCHARD, FLYING AN ARGENTINE FLAG, ANCHORED HIS FLEET WHILE RAIDING THE MISSION.

HISTORICAL LANDMARK NO 189

CALIFORNIA STATE PARK COMMISSION

▲ One of the few natural harbors along the Southern California coast, Dana Point is a designated historical landmark.

▶ To ensure the Spanish coastal village look he envisioned, Ole Hanson, San Clemente's founding father, required that all building plans be submitted for review.

◄ Railroad tracks run the length of the shoreline
in San Clemente, along the nation's second-busiest rail corridor.
▲ Rocky promontories, a creek running from the foothills, and long, sandy stretches
of shore make Aliso Beach one of Southern California's most appealing recreational areas.
►► Typically foggy in summer and clear in winter, the Southern California sunshine
burns off the coastal cloud cover, revealing pleasure boats off Balboa Island.

◀ There is no mystery as to why Franciscan monks chose this
Mediterranean Eden as the site for the Mission at San Juan Capistrano.
▲ Founded in November 1776 and named for Italian theologian St. John of
Capistrano (1386–1456), this architectural jewel and the seventh
of the California missions prospered from the start.

▲ Landscaped with old-world roses,
bougainvillea, and lavender, the mission gardens and
arcaded walkways capture the romance of California's Spanish heritage.
▶ Still in use today, the first small chapel was built in 1777. Called
the "Serra Chapel," it is the only existing building where
Father Junípero Serra celebrated mass.

◄ Beyond Corona del Mar's exclusive residential streets, named after fruits and
flowers, are many of Orange County's most treasured locations: the tide pools at Big
Corona Beach, China Cove, Lookout Point, Inspiration Point, and Little Corona Beach.
▲ Quaint homes accented by unique decorations line Balboa Island's Grand Canal,
the narrow waterway that separates the main island and Little Balboa Island.
►► Visitors from around the world come to lose themselves in the lush,
meditative gardens of San Juan Capistrano's mission.

▲ Now largely within the Cleveland
National Forest, Trabuco Canyon is home
to native sycamore, oaks, and pine, as
well as songbirds and wildflowers.

▲ A riot of flowers brightens the
mission grounds at San Juan Capistrano.
▶▶ Every day comes to a perfect end along the
American Riviera—the unparalleled coastline
of Orange County's golden shores.